AMAZING INVENTORY OF INCREDIBLE KNOWLEDGE

★

PUB TIME

TRIVIA

Publications International, Ltd.

Written by Christopher Lagerstrom & Jill Oldham

Cover photo: Shutterstock.com

Louis Weber, CEO
Publications International, Ltd.
8140 Lehigh Avenue
Morton Grove, Illinois 60053

ISBN: 978-1-68022-712-3

Manufactured in China.

8 7 6 5 4 3 2 1

CONTENTS

TRIVIA TIME

Welcome to *Pub Time Trivia*. This is not your typical trivia book. If you're looking for dry and dusty historical trivia, you won't find it here. But if you think you know—or always wanted to know—how to measure the hotness of chilies, where to find the most poisonous animal in the world, what an octothorpe is, and many more attention-grabbing facts, you've come to the right place.

Pub Time Trivia is organized by topic, making it easy for you to pick your favorite category. Perhaps you win the office Oscar pool every year and would like to premiere with Movie Mania. Or you could tempt yourself with Food & Drink, or find out about Famous Firsts. You'll find questions on the right-hand pages and answers on the back of each page, along with a few extra tidbits that may teach you a thing or two.

Are you ready? Pull up a barstool, pull out *Pub Time Trivia*, and tell your friends the next trivia champion has arrived.

1. WHICH OF THESE DOG BREEDS CANNOT BARK?

A. Azawakh

B. Basenji

C. Catalburun

D. Mudi

2. INSECT STINGS KILL BETWEEN 40 AND 100 AMERICANS EVERY YEAR. BUT IN OTHER PARTS OF THE WORLD, BUGS KILL MANY TIMES THAT NUMBER. WHICH OF THESE CRITTERS IS RESPONSIBLE FOR THE MOST HUMAN DEATHS?

A. Assassin bug

B. Japanese beetle

C. Mosquito

D. Tsetse fly

1.

B. Basenjis, a favorite dog of ancient Egyptians, are incapable of barking. Instead, you'll hear them uttering a sound called a yodel. Azawakhs (African sight hounds), catalburuns (Turkish pointers that are readily identified by their "split-nose"), and mudis (Hungarian herding dogs) all make themselves heard with traditional barks.

2.

C. Believe it or not, mosquitoes are responsible for more deaths than any other creature in the world. They spread a wide variety of potentially deadly diseases, including malaria, which kills an estimated one million people a year.

3. WHAT IS A CAPON?

A. A castrated rooster

B. A pygmy giraffe

C. A wild dog

D. An unfertilized eagle egg

4. WHAT PART OF A HORSE IS KNOWN AS THE "FROG"?

A. Chest

B. Head

C. Hoof

D. Tail

5. WHAT TYPE OF ANIMAL IS A HOLSTEIN?

A. Cow

B. Horse

C. Pig

D. Sheep

6. TRUE OR FALSE?

The sting from a killer bee can be fatal.

3.

A. Ouch. Why would a rooster be castrated? To improve the tenderness and quality of its meat. Capon is known as a luxury food.

4.

C. The frog is the triangular mark on the bottom of a horse's hoof.

5.

A. Got milk? Black-and-white (or sometimes red-and-white) Holsteins are the most popular dairy cows in the United States, making up 90 percent of the total herd.

6.

True. Africanized honeybees, as killer bees are officially known, are extremely aggressive. They often attack in swarms, and their stings can kill. They are notorious for being easy to provoke and hard to escape. They will chase humans for great distances, and they've been known to stay angry for up to 24 hours.

7. **WHICH SPECIES CONTAINS THE MOST POISONOUS ANIMAL IN THE WORLD?**

A. Butterfly

B. Frog

C. Snake

D. Spider

8. **MOST PEOPLE KNOW THAT A GROUP OF LIONS IS CALLED A PRIDE AND A GROUP OF FISH IS CALLED A SCHOOL, BUT CAN YOU MATCH THESE ANIMALS WITH THEIR COLLECTIVE GROUP NAMES?**

1. Apes	**A.** Murder
2. Crows	**B.** Parliament
3. Jellyfish	**C.** Pod
4. Owls	**D.** Shrewdness
5. Ravens	**E.** Smack
6. Whales	**F.** Unkindness

9. **WHAT IS STORED INSIDE A CAMEL'S HUMP?**

7.

B. Dart poison frogs are the most poisonous animals in the world. The golden poison frog is so toxic that it's dangerous to even touch it. Just one golden poison frog has enough toxin to kill ten people. So if you find yourself in Central or South America, you might want to think twice before kissing that frog.

8.

1. D; 2. A; 3. E; 4. B; 5. F; 6. C.

9.

Fat. If you thought the answer was water, you're not alone. (You're wrong, but you're not alone.) The fat stored in a camel's hump allows the animal to go for up to a month without food—pretty useful for those long treks across the desert.

10. **WHICH OF THE FOLLOWING ANIMALS WAS NEVER A RESIDENT OF THE WHITE HOUSE?**

A. Alligator

B. Bobcat

C. Ostrich

D. Pygmy hippopotamus

11. **MACARONI, GENTOO, CHINSTRAP, AND ROCKHOPPER ARE TYPES OF WHAT?**

A. Butterflies

B. Dogs

C. Penguins

D. Zebras

12. **WHICH OF THE FOLLOWING IS NOT A TYPE OF CAT?**

A. Calico

B. Rex

C. Saluki

D. Scottish Fold

10.

C. The White House has been home to all sorts of animals—domesticated and otherwise. John Quincy Adams owned a gator that lived in the East Room for two months. Calvin Coolidge literally had a zoo at the White House, including a bobcat, a pygmy hippo, a bear, lion cubs, raccoons, a hyena, and more. Theodore Roosevelt had an extensive menagerie too.

11.

C. There are 17 breeds of penguins in the world; these are just four of them.

12.

C. Salukis are dogs—in fact, theirs may be the oldest known breed of domesticated dog. Salukis were held in such great esteem in ancient Egypt that they were sometimes mummified along with the pharaohs.

13. OF THE 12 SIGNS OF THE ZODIAC, HOW MANY ARE MODELED ON ANIMALS?

14. WHAT DO SNAKES PRIMARILY USE THEIR TONGUES FOR?

    A. Hearing

    B. Seeing

    C. Smelling

    D. Tasting

15. ON AVERAGE, WHICH OF THE FOLLOWING SHARK SPECIES KILLS THE MOST HUMANS EACH YEAR?

    A. Copper shark

    B. Bull shark

    C. Tiger shark

    D. Mako shark

13.

Seven. Aries (ram), Taurus (bull), Cancer (crab), Leo (lion), Scorpio (scorpion), Capricorn (sea goat), and Pisces (fish) are animal signs.

14.

C. While snakes can use their tongues for tasting and even touching, they use them mostly for smelling.

15.

B. The United States averages fewer than one shark fatality every two years, while an average of 39 people are killed each year by lightning strikes. Statistically, you should be more afraid of the turf than the surf.

16. **THE PANGOLIN, A TOOTHLESS MAMMAL FOUND IN SOUTHERN AFRICA AND ASIA, IS THE ONLY MAMMAL TO HAVE WHICH OF THE FOLLOWING REPTILIAN CHARACTERISTICS?**

A. Can grow back its tail

B. Has scales

C. Is cold blooded

D. Secretes venom

17. **EXCLUDING INSECTS, WHICH ANIMAL HAS THE FASTEST METABOLISM?**

A. Cheetah

B. Pygmy shrew

C. Hummingbird

D. Chipmunk

18. **TRUE OR FALSE?**

A jellyfish has no brain.

16.

B. The pangolin, sometimes referred to as the scaly anteater, is the only mammal with scales. It has no teeth, and uses its powerful claws to tear open termite and ant mounds.

17.

C. Hummingbirds, which consume more than their own body weight in nectar daily, are always mere hours away from starvation. With an average heart rate of 1,260 beats per minute, a hummingbird can slow its heart down to 50 to 180 beats per minute, allowing it to survive when food is scarce. Second place in the high metabolism race goes to the eternally hungry Eurasian pygmy shrew, which can go only ten minutes without eating.

18.

True. The jellyfish has no brain, blood, or nervous system. Jellyfish do have eyespots that can detect light and dark, as well as chemosensory pits that can identify potential predators. And don't let their name fool you—jellyfish are 95% water.

ARTS & LITERATURE

1. TO WHICH INVENTOR DID HELEN KELLER DEDICATE HER AUTOBIOGRAPHY AFTER HE HAD ACTED AS A TUTOR TO HER?

A. Alexander Graham Bell

B. Thomas Edison

C. Antonio Meucci

D. Elisha Gray

2. IN ROALD DAHL'S CHILDREN'S BOOK OF THE SAME NAME, TO WHAT DOES *THE BFG* REFER?

A. Belly Flop Gang

B. Best Friends Guild

C. Brain Freeze Gulp

D. Big Friendly Giant

1.

A. Keller dedicated her autobiography *The Story of My Life* to the man who invented the first practical telephone, the metal detector, and the hydrofoil.

2.

D. Standing 24 feet tall, the BFG's main job was to deliver good dreams to children. He first appeared in Dahl's *Danny, the Champion of the World*. Too bad he didn't show up in Dahl's James Bond script *You Only Live Twice*.

3. **WHICH OF THE FOLLOWING CHARACTERS NEVER APPEARED IN J.R.R. TOLKIEN'S _THE LORD OF THE RINGS_ TRILOGY?**

A. Meriadoc

B. Ahsoka

C. Faramir

D. Elrond

4. **WHAT DISTINGUISHES FRENCH PAINTER MONET FROM FRENCH PAINTER MANET, ASIDE FROM THE VOWEL IN THEIR NAMES? MATCH EACH FACT TO ONE OF THE PAINTERS.**

A. Painted outdoor scenes and people while in a studio

B. Painted what he saw while outdoors

C. Was married twice and tried to commit suicide in between marriages

D. Married his father's mistress and died from rheumatism, gangrene, and syphilis

ARTS & LITERATURE

QUESTIONS

3.

B. Meriadoc was the Hobbit better known as Merry, Faramir was the human Boromir's brother, and Elrond was the elf lord. Ahsoka is Anakin Skywalker's apprentice in the TV show *Star Wars: The Clone Wars*...and maybe the future movies?

4.

Claude Monet was fond of painting outdoor scenes (**B**) and was married twice (**C**); Monet tried to end it all because he wasn't making money, but at the end of his life he did all right for himself. Edouard Manet primarily painted while indoors (**A**) and had an unpleasant demise (**D**); it's even possible that Manet's son might actually have been his brother.

5. RICHARD BACHMAN IS THE ALTER EGO OF WHICH FAMOUS AUTHOR?

A. Stephen King

B. John Grisham

C. Tom Wolfe

D. John Updike

6. IN RAY BRADBURY'S *FAHRENHEIT 451*, BOOKS ARE SO ILLEGAL THAT, IF YOU'RE FOUND WITH ONE, FIREFIGHTERS WILL BURN DOWN YOUR HOUSE. WHICH OF THESE BOOKS DIDN'T RAY BRADBURY WRITE?

A. *Dandelion Wine*

B. *The Martian Chronicles*

C. *The Door into Summer*

D. *Something Wicked This Way Comes*

7. WHAT DOES THE "J" STAND FOR IN AUTHOR J. K. ROWLING'S NAME?

A. Jane

B. Joanne

C. Joely

D. Judy

5.

A. King chose the name Richard after crime novelist Donald E. Westlake's pseudonym, Richard Stark, and Bachman for the band Bachman-Turner Overdrive. He started writing under the pen name to test whether it was his talent or his name that sold books. He wrote four novels (*Rage*, *The Long Walk*, *Roadwork*, and *The Running Man*) before being discovered. King continues to reference his most lifelike creation to this day.

6.

C. *The Door into Summer* was written by Bradbury contemporary Robert A. Heinlein in 1956. Bradbury's seasonally titled *Farewell Summer* was published in 2006; Bradbury passed away six years later. Farewell, Ray.

7.

B. The initials stand for Joanne Kathleen, but the *Harry Potter* author usually goes by "Jo."

8. *DESTINO* IS A WALT DISNEY-PRODUCED ANIMATED SHORT FILM RELEASED IN 2003. ITS ACTUAL PRODUCTION BEGAN IN 1945 AND FEATURED WORK BY DISNEY HIMSELF AND WHAT FAMOUS ARTIST?

A. Salvador Dali

B. Pablo Picasso

C. Henri Matisse

D. Max Ernst

9. WHO SCULPTED THE FAMOUS STATUE DAVID, SUPPOSEDLY THE REPRESENTATION OF THE IDEAL MALE BODY?

A. Botticelli

B. Michelangelo

C. Francesco da Sangallo

D. Leonardo da Vinci

10. WHICH AUTHOR CREATED THE LAND OF OZ?

A. Roald Dahl

B. J.R.R. Tolkien

C. L. Frank Baum

D. C. S. Lewis

8.

A. While preparing for *Fantasia 2000*, Walt's nephew Roy E. Disney stumbled across the unfinished project and championed its completion. Disney added computer animation alongside the original footage. It's a meeting of the generations. A true Surrealist moment. It was...*Destino*.

9.

B. Take that, Mike "the Situation." You may think you have abs of steel, but David has equally well-sculpted abs of marble—and he's more than 500 years old.

10.

C. Oz stemmed from Baum's imagination, but the other writers also created some pretty fantastical worlds: Dahl came up with Willy Wonka's chocolate factory (among others), Tolkien is responsible for Middle-earth of *Lord of the Rings*, and Lewis dreamed up Narnia.

11. ARCHITECT ANTONI GAUDÍ WAS CONSIDERED A *MODERNISTA*. HE WAS INSPIRED BY THE SHAPES OF TREE TRUNKS AND HUMAN BONES AS WELL AS THE CLASSIC GOTHIC STYLE, AND HE INCORPORATED ALL THREE INTO HIS DESIGNS. IN WHICH COUNTRY WILL YOU FIND HIS WORK?

A. France

B. Spain

C. Turkey

D. Italy

12. OPRAH WINFREY FAMOUSLY GOT INTO A FIGHT WITH WHICH AUTHOR ON HER TALK SHOW?

A. Dave Eggers

B. Jonathan Franzen

C. James Frey

D. Jonathan Safran Foer

13. WHICH BOOK USES EXACTLY 50 DIFFERENT WORDS?

11.

B. Do one of two things immediately. Check out the amazing photographs of his buildings online— or fly to Barcelona, Spain.

12.

C. When Oprah discovered that the author of the self-purported memoir *A Million Little Pieces* had lied about parts of his life in the novel, she was outraged. She said she felt "duped" and proceeded to give him a very public verbal whoopin'.

13.

Dr. Seuss's *Green Eggs and Ham*. Seuss's editor bet him he couldn't write a book using 50 words or less. Guess what? The editor lost.

14. WHO DESIGNED THE GUGGENHEIM MUSEUM IN NEW YORK CITY?

A. Frank Gehry

B. Louis Kahn

C. Ludwig Mies van der Rohe

D. Frank Lloyd Wright

15. ON WHICH SURFACE WOULD YOU FIND A TRADITIONAL FRESCO?

A. A canvas

B. A piece of pottery

C. Skin

D. A wall

16. MATCH THESE ARTISTS WITH THE MOVEMENT WITH WHICH THEY ARE MOST ASSOCIATED:

1. Salvador Dali	**A.** Cubism
2. Henri Matisse	**B.** Impressionism
3. Mary Cassatt	**C.** Pop Art
4. Pablo Picasso	**D.** Fauvism
5. Andy Warhol	**E.** Surrealism

27

14.

D. The renowned modern-art museum showcased both Wright's affinity for the natural world and his later take on modernist architecture. It opened in 1959, after the death of both Wright and art collector Solomon Guggenheim.

15.

D. A fresco (which means "fresh" in Italian) is a mural painted on fresh, wet plaster with natural pigments. As the plaster and paint dry, the fresco hardens and becomes permanent. Frescoes are commonly found on church walls.

16.

1. E; 2. D; 3. B; 4. A; 5. C.

17. WHO WROTE *PRIDE AND PREJUDICE*?

A. Jane Austen

B. Elizabeth Bennet

C. Charlotte Brontë

D. Emily Brontë

18. ACCORDING TO GREEK LEGEND, WHAT WAS LEFT IN PANDORA'S BOX AFTER SHE OPENED IT, RELEASING MISERY AND EVIL INTO THE WORLD?

A. Faith

B. Hope

C. Innocence

D. Trust

19. WHAT COLOR IS THE ARTS AND LITERATURE WEDGE IN THE GAME TRIVIAL PURSUIT?

17.

A. Austen wrote the widely beloved novel. The Brontë sisters contributed *Jane Eyre* (Charlotte) and *Wuthering Heights* (Emily) to the genre. Elizabeth Bennet is a figment of Austen's imagination—the main character in *Pride and Prejudice*.

18.

B. Tricky Zeus. The king of gods gave Pandora a box (well, technically it was a jar, but why quibble?) and warned her never, ever to open it. Of course he knew her curiosity would get the better of her, and indeed it did. Fortunately she was able to slam the lid shut while hope still remained.

19.

Brown. (Talk about trivial trivia!)

1. WHICH U.S. PRESIDENT FIRST CHOSE TO FLY IN A PRIVATE U.S. AIR FORCE PLANE INSTEAD OF ON COMMERCIAL AIRLINES?

A. Harry S. Truman

B. John F. Kennedy

C. Franklin D. Roosevelt

D. Dwight D. Eisenhower

2. WHO WAS THE FIRST PERSON BORN IN THE AMERICAS TO ENGLISH PARENTS?

A. John Truth

B. Virginia Dare

C. Sarah Delaware

D. John Maine

1.

C. The practice of using a private U.S. Air Force plane for the president of the United States was instituted in 1943, after concerns arose over the president's security while flying commercial. The president's plane, known today as *Air Force One*, was originally called *Sacred Cow*. The name had to be changed in 1953 after the president's plane shared airspace with a commercial airliner going by the same call sign.

2.

B. Virginia Dare, the first baby born in the Americas to English parents, was born in the Roanoke Colony in present-day North Carolina. Virginia's birth is known only because her grandfather, John White, returned to England for fresh supplies and spread the news of his new granddaughter. Upon his return to Roanoke, he discovered that the entire colony, including his granddaughter, had mysteriously disappeared.

3. WHO WAS MAJOR LEAGUE BASEBALL'S FIRST ROOKIE OF THE YEAR?

A. Lou Gehrig

B. Babe Ruth

C. Honus Wagner

D. Jackie Robinson

4. WHICH MUSICIAN WAS FIRST TO HAVE A NUMBER-ONE HIT ON THE BILLBOARD HOT 100 FOR A SONG THAT FEATURED ONLY PIANO AND VOCALS?

A. Billy Joel

B. Elton John

C. Mariah Carey

D. Adele

5. WHO WAS THE COVER MODEL OF THE FIRST ISSUE OF *PLAYBOY* MAGAZINE (1953)?

A. Brigitte Bardot

B. Sophia Loren

C. Jayne Mansfield

D. Marilyn Monroe

3.

D. In 1947, Jackie Robinson won the very first Rookie of the Year award. The award was originally called The J. Louis Comiskey Award after the longtime owner of the Chicago White Sox. The award was renamed The Jackie Robinson Award in 1987, 40 years after Jackie Robinson suited up as a Brooklyn Dodger and broke baseball's color barrier.

4.

D. In 2011, Adele's "Someone Like You" became the first single ever to reach the number one spot on the charts with piano and vocals exclusively. "Candle in the Wind 1997," Elton John's tribute song to Princess Diana, topped the charts for 14 weeks in 1997—if it weren't for that pesky orchestra at the end.

5.

D. Monroe was also the centerfold of that issue.

6. WHAT 1970S FILM WAS THE FIRST TO FEATURE A COMPUTER-GENERATED TITLE SEQUENCE?

A. *Jaws 2*

B. *Revenge of the Pink Panther*

C. *Grease*

D. *Superman*

7. WHO WAS *TIME* MAGAZINE'S VERY FIRST MAN OF THE YEAR?

A. Mahatma Gandhi

B. Adolf Hitler

C. Charles Lindbergh

D. Albert Einstein

8. WHICH SHOW WAS THE FIRST EVER TO WIN A TONY AWARD FOR BEST MUSICAL?

A. *Kiss Me, Kate*

B. *South Pacific*

C. *Guys & Dolls*

D. *The King and I*

6.

D. *Superman* became the first of many films to use computer animation in its opening sequence. Released in 1978, *Superman*'s production preceded a boom in digital filmmaking by only a few years (the CGI-heavy *Tron* was released in 1982). As such, the film's creative team had to manufacture a 70-foot scale model of the Golden Gate Bridge, as well as one for the Hoover Dam.

7.

C. Charles Lindbergh was an easy pick for the first *Time* magazine Man of the Year in 1927—and not just because *Time* forgot to put him on its cover earlier that year when he completed the world's first transatlantic flight.

8.

A. The first Tony Awards were given out in 1947, but until 1949, there was no category for Best Musical. In 1949, *Kiss Me, Kate*, based on William Shakespeare's *The Taming of The Shrew*, took the inaugural honors for a new musical. New rule: "If you want an award, always bet on Shakespeare."

9. WHICH WAS THE FIRST RECURRING CHARACTER TO BE KILLED OFF BY THE MAKERS OF LONG-RUNNING ANIMATED TV SERIES *THE SIMPSONS*?

A. Maude Flanders

B. Sideshow Bob

C. Bleeding Gums Murphy

D. Dr. Julius M. Hibbert

10. THE FIRST CREDIT CARD WAS INTRODUCED IN NEW YORK IN 1950. WHAT WAS IT?

A. American Express

B. BankAmericard

C. Diners Club

D. MasterCard

11. THE FIRST MOVING PICTURE COPYRIGHTED IN AMERICA SHOWED WHAT?

A. An automobile racing a horse

B. A lady crossing a street

C. A man sneezing

D. Two people kissing

9.

C. After long debates about offing a character, the makers of *The Simpsons* finally pulled the trigger in Season Six, when they killed off Lisa Simpson's idol, jazz musician Bleeding Gums Murphy. Bleeding Gums Murphy appeared to Lisa one last time in the form of a speaking cloud, alongside Darth Vader of *Star Wars* and Mufasa from *The Lion King*, characters originally voiced by James Earl Jones, who reprised his roles for the cartoon.

10.

C. Although the American Express company was established a century before Diners Club, it specialized in deliveries (as a competitor to the U.S. Postal Service), money orders, and traveler's checks. It didn't enter the credit card industry until 1958.

11.

C. The five-second movie, filmed in 1894 by the Edison Manufacturing Company (yes, that Edison— he did a lot more than invent the lightbulb), showed Edison's assistant Fred Ott taking a pinch of snuff and sneezing. Five stars!

12. SEEING A NEED FOR A STORE WHERE YOU COULD BUY MILK, BREAD, AND EGGS AFTER REGULAR GROCERY STORES CLOSED FOR THE NIGHT, "UNCLE" JOHNNY JEFFERSON GREEN OPENED THE VERY FIRST AFTER-HOURS CONVENIENCE STORE, WHICH EVOLVED INTO A CHAIN OF STORES KNOWN WORLDWIDE AS 7-ELEVEN. WHAT DID GREEN ORIGINALLY CALL HIS STORE?

A. Uncle Johnny's Icehouse

B. Tote'm

C. Stop and Go

D. Jefferson General

13. WHAT WAS THE FIRST ITEM SOLD ON EBAY?

A. Answering machine

B. Calculator

C. Computer keyboard

D. Laser pointer

12.

B. Tote'm stores were named for how customers could simply buy goods and "tote 'em" away. Many of the first Tote'm stores even had original Alaskan totem poles out front. In 1946, the chain changed its name to 7-Eleven to let customers know about their newly extended hours.

13.

D. eBay was founded in 1995 by Pierre Omidyar, whose broken laser pointer was the first product to be auctioned off (reportedly for about $14). The buyer was aware it was broken—he wanted it as an addition to his collection of broken laser pointers. True story.

14. **WHO WAS THE FIRST HUMAN IN SPACE?**

A. Yuri Gagarin

B. John Glenn

C. Alan Shepard

D. German Titov

15. **WHAT WAS THE FIRST ANIMATED FILM TO BE NOMINATED FOR AN ACADEMY AWARD FOR BEST PICTURE?**

A. *Aladdin*

B. *Beauty and the Beast*

C. *The Lion King*

D. *The Little Mermaid*

16. **WHAT WAS THE FIRST VIDEO EVER PLAYED ON MTV?**

A. "Beat It," Michael Jackson

B. "Money for Nothing," Dire Straits

C. "Paradise by the Dashboard Light," Meat Loaf

D. "Video Killed the Radio Star," The Buggles

41

14.

A. The Russian cosmonaut launched aboard the *Vostok 1* on April 12, 1961, and orbited the Earth once. The spacecraft was controlled from the ground for the duration of the 108-minute flight. Gagarin was its only passenger.

15.

B. *Beauty and the Beast* was nominated in 1991 but was beaten out by *The Silence of the Lambs*. However, it did win the Golden Globe for Best Picture (Musical or Comedy) that year—the first full-length animated feature to claim that prize.

16.

D. At midnight on August 1, 1981, MTV launched with the airing of the music video of the Buggles' 1979 debut single. Irony at its finest.

1. BEFORE BECOMING BABY RUTH IN 1921, WHAT WAS THE CANDY BAR'S ORIGINAL NAME?

A. Nuts N' Nougat

B. The ChocoBar

C. Caramel Surprise

D. Kandy Kake

2. WHEN HOSTESS DECLARED BANKRUPTCY IN 2012, THE FUTURE FOR TWINKIES DIDN'T LOOK SO CREAMY. WHICH COMPANY HAS SAVED THE GOLDEN CAKE FROM BECOMING HISTORY?

A. Nabisco

B. Apollo

C. Little Debbie

D. Pepperidge Farm

1.

D. Already successful in Chicago, the Curtiss Candy Company thought the redesigned bar needed a new name. The company claimed the change had nothing to do with Babe Ruth's rise in fame. They claimed it was named after President Grover Cleveland's daughter, Ruth. Cleveland had been president 30 years prior, and his daughter Ruth had passed away in 1904 at the age of 12. A clever marketing move to get around licensing, or simple truth? It didn't matter to Nabisco, who bought the company 60 years later, or Nestlé, who owns them today.

2.

B. One of these things is not like the other. Apollo is a global management firm that owns the likes of AMC Entertainment, Norwegian Cruise Lines, and Carl's Jr. Hopefully, with Apollo's help, Twinkies *can* last forever.

3. WHAT IS THE ONLY FOOD THAT, WHEN SEALED, DOESN'T SPOIL?

A. Beer nuts

B. Capers

C. Fruit preserves

D. Honey

4. TRUE OR FALSE?

It takes seven years to digest swallowed gum.

5. THE MCDONALD'S BIG MAC IS BY FAR THE CHAIN'S BIGGEST HIT. BUT STANDING IN STARK CONTRAST TO THAT SANDWICH ARE SOME WACKY OFFERINGS. WHICH OF THESE WAS NOT A REAL MENU ITEM FROM THE FAST-FOOD BEHEMOTH?

A. McCrepe

B. McGratin Croquette

C. McLobster

D. McPizza

3.

D. Airtight containers will make honey last forever—literally! Several giant vats of honey, untouched for more than 3,000 years, were excavated from King Tut's tomb. Incredibly, the honey was found to still be edible.

4.

False. Although gum is indigestible, it passes through your digestive system at a normal rate.

5.

A. You won't find a crepe on any Mickey D's menu past or present, but the other three have all been featured at some point. What's in a McGratin Croquette, you ask? The Japanese-market sandwich featured fried macaroni, shrimp, and mashed potatoes. Are you lovin' it?

6. WHAT DOES THE SCOVILLE SCALE MEASURE?

A. The fattiness of a cut of meat

B. The purity of olive oil

C. The "heat" of chilies

D. The clarity of wine

7. M&Ms AND GATORADE COME IN A RAINBOW OF COLORS THANKS TO MYRIAD ARTIFICIAL DYES. RESEARCHERS HAVE FOUND THAT ONE OF THESE COLORS OF DYES MAY HELP CURE SPINAL CORD INJURIES. DO YOU KNOW WHICH ONE?

8. ACCORDING TO THE U.S. FOOD AND DRUG ADMINISTRATION (FDA), MOST RAW FRUITS AND VEGETABLES ARE COMPLETELY FAT-FREE. WHICH IS THE EXCEPTION TO THIS RULE?

A. Bananas

B. Broccoli

C. Jicama

D. Plums

6.

C. Are you feeling hot, hot, hot? The Scoville scale can either confirm or refute your hotness.

7.

Blue. Researchers discovered that an injection of the dye Brilliant Blue G halted the chemical reaction that destroys spinal tissue after an injury. Better yet, after the dye was injected into rats paralyzed from spinal cord injuries, they were able to walk again. The only side effect? They temporarily turned blue.

8.

B. If you zeroed in on broccoli, you're correct. While the others have zero fat, broccoli has a whole—*gasp*—.5 grams per stalk. (Still pretty healthy, no? Doesn't that make you want to put down those nachos and Buffalo wings?)

9. **WHICH PRODUCT WAS ORIGINALLY MARKETED AS "ESTEEMED BRAIN TONIC AND INTELLECTUAL BEVERAGE"?**

A. Coca-Cola

B. Maxwell House coffee

C. Schweppes ginger ale

D. Smart Water

10. **CLAMSHELL, TABLE, BLACK TRUMPET, AND GOLDEN NEEDLE ARE ALL TYPES OF WHAT?**

A. Figs

B. Mushrooms

C. Pears

D. Snails

11. **WHICH OF THESE SWEET TREATS HAS NOT BEEN FEATURED AS A MAIN INGREDIENT IN A BREAKFAST CEREAL?**

A. AirHeads

B. Ice cream

C. Raisinets

D. Willy Wonka's Nerds candy

9.

A. Coca-Cola was invented in Atlanta, Georgia, where it debuted in 1886 and sold for five cents a glass.

10.

B. If you see any of these varieties, feel free to yell, "There's a fungus among us!" (Although people might look at you funny.)

11.

C. Although sugar-happy tykes everywhere might think Raisin Bran could be improved by coating the raisins with chocolate, no such cereal has been created...yet. Cap'n Crunch's AirHeads Berries was produced by Quaker in 2003. In 1965 Kellogg's introduced Kream Krunch, which was filled with bits of freeze-dried ice cream. And the tangy flavor of Nerds candy was recreated in Nerds Cereal in the mid-1980s, with Ralston cleverly dividing the cereal box in half to feature a different flavor in each compartment, just like the candy box.

12. EACH YEAR, PEOPLE CELEBRATE LOCAL FOOD SPECIALTIES WITH GIANT FESTIVALS. IF YOU'RE TIRED OF THE SAME OLD CHILI COOK-OFF OR APPLE PIE CONTEST, YOU MAY WANT TO CHECK ONE OF THESE OUT. ALL BUT ONE IS A REAL FESTIVAL—WHICH IS THE ODD MAN OUT?

A. Jelly Jam-boree

B. Turkey Testicle Festival

C. Waikiki SPAM Jam West

D. Virginia Roadkill Cook-off

13. TRUE OR FALSE?

Eating turkey makes people sleepy.

14. NATURAL VANILLA FLAVORING COMES FROM WHICH FLOWER?

A. Calla lily

B. Dahlia

C. Orchid

D. Sweet pea

12.

A. If you find yourself with a craving for some turkey testicles, drop by Huntley, Illinois, in November. For roadkill delicacies, head to Pocahontas County, West Virginia, in September. And if you like canned meat, you're in luck—every April. Alas, if you're looking to sample jellies and jams, you may have to start your own festival.

13.

False. Turkey contains tryptophan—an amino acid that makes people sleepy—but it doesn't work unless it's consumed in large quantities.

14.

C. Vanilla pods, or beans, are the fruit of the vanilla orchid—the only orchid plant that produces an edible fruit. Now, if only chocolate grew on trees... Wait a minute—it does! Cacao pods, which are used to make chocolate, grow on small tropical trees called Theobroma cacao trees.

15. AMERICANS DRINK 13 BILLION GALLONS OF SOFT DRINKS EVERY YEAR. WHICH OF THE FOLLOWING IS NOT A REAL PRODUCT?

A. DraCola

B. EpilepsiPepsi

C. Leninade

D. Whooppee Soda

16. WHAT IS THE ONLY ROCK THAT IS EDIBLE FOR HUMANS?

17. TOFU (OR *DOUFU*, AS IT WOULD MORE ACCURATELY BE SPELLED IN CHINA) IS A STAPLE OF ASIAN COOKING, AND IT HAS MADE INROADS IN NORTH AMERICAN CUISINE BECAUSE OF ITS HIGH PROTEIN AND CALCIUM CONTENT. IT IS MADE FROM SOYBEANS; IN FACT, *DOU* MEANS "BEANS." BUT WHAT DOES THE *FU* TRANSLATE AS?

A. Curd

B. Rotten

C. Silk

D. Vegan

15.

B. There's no such thing as EpilepsiPepsi. The other three were all actual soft drinks. DraCola was a cola product made for "Halloween fans of all ages" by Transylvania Imports. Leninade was humorously promoted with slogans like, "A taste worth standing in line for," and "A drink for the masses!" And Whooppee Soda was a ginger ale–flavored soda marketed as "The Bottled Joy."

16.

Salt. The mineral is essential to the body, but consuming too much is not good for you. No surprise there. But did you know that it can be deadly? An overdose of salt was a traditional method of suicide in ancient China.

17.

B. Mmmm-mm, "rotten beans." No wonder tofu has a bad rap!

GRAB BAG

1. ALTHOUGH IT'S RARE ON EARTH, WHAT IS THE SECOND-MOST ABUNDANT ELEMENT IN THE KNOWN UNIVERSE?

2. AN INTERROBANG IS MADE BY COMBINING WHAT TWO PUNCTUATION MARKS?

    A. ! and ?

    B. > and <

    C.) and (

    D. : and %

3. WHAT SYMBOL IS ALSO KNOWN AS AN OCTOTHORPE?

4. LIST ALL EIGHT VEGETABLES IN THE ORIGINAL RECIPE FOR **V8** JUICE.

QUESTIONS

1.

Helium. Earth is running out of helium, which is mostly mined from the ground. Helium conservationists seek to multiply its price by 20 times to stop wasteful use. Look out, gold, there's a new precious commodity in town—save those birthday balloons!

2.

A. Invented in 1962 by advertiser Martin Spektor, the combination expresses surprise in a question. Through the early 1970s, the key could be found on typewriters or as an add-on, but the fad faded away like a forgotten pet rock.

3.

You may know it as the pound, number, or hashtag sign. For the record, the asterisk (*) is also known as a sextile.

4.

Beets, carrots, celery, lettuce, parsley, spinach, tomatoes, and watercress.

5. A 2013 DOCUMENTARY ENTITLED *SIRIUS* IS ABOUT THE ATACAMA HUMANOID DISCOVERED IN A DESERT IN CHILE IN 2003. WHAT'S SO UNIQUE ABOUT THE HUMANOID NICKNAMED ATA?

A. It has a full-length, prehensile tail.

B. It's been fully preserved for more than 500 years.

C. It's six inches tall.

D. It has wings instead of arms.

6. LEGO BRICKS WERE INTRODUCED IN WHAT DECADE?

A. 1930s

B. 1940s

C. 1950s

D. 1960s

7. MOUND METALCRAFT, FOUNDED IN 1946, CHANGED ITS NAME IN 1955, AND ITS NEW NAME BECAME SYNONYMOUS WITH A CERTAIN TYPE OF TOY TRUCK. WHAT WAS THE COMPANY'S NEW NAME?

5.

C. Are you Sirius? The public has speculated that Ata is an extraterrestrial, but DNA testing determined it's human after all.

6.

C. LEGO creator Ole Kirk Christansen named his wooden toys factory after a fusion of the Danish words "leg" and "godt," literally meaning "play well." The plastic bricks were perfected in the 1950s, and a new LEGO brick will fit one made in 1958. I guess you could say they still stack up against themselves.

7.

Tonka. The name came from the Dakota Sioux word *tanka*, meaning "great" or "big." Tonka has almost become a proprietary eponym, like Xerox or Kleenex, when referring to toy trucks.

8. **WHICH IS THE ONLY KING CARD IN A STANDARD DECK OF PLAYING CARDS WITHOUT A MOUSTACHE?**

A. King of Diamonds

B. King of Hearts

C. King of Spades

D. King of Clubs

9. **WHAT IS THE STATUE OF LIBERTY'S OFFICIAL NAME?**

A. Lady Liberty on the Isle

B. Light of Liberty, Let It Shine

C. Liberty Gertrude Ellis

D. Liberty Enlightening the World

10. **WHAT IS NOT A POSSIBLE ANSWER FROM THE MAGIC 8-BALL?**

A. As I see it, yes

B. Better not tell you now

C. I don't think so

D. Without a doubt

8.

B. Because he also holds his sword behind (or through) his head, the King of Hearts is also called the suicide king. Did you know that each card represents a famous king? The King of Diamonds is Julius Caesar or Caesar Augustus, Clubs is Alexander the Great, Spades is King David of Israel, and Hearts is Charlemagne.

9.

D. Given to us by France in 1886, she's become quite the movie star. At her worst, she's appeared in such features as *Independence Day*, *The Day After Tomorrow*, *Judge Dredd*, *A.I.*, *X-Men*, *Cloverfield*, and of course, *Planet of the Apes*. At her best: *Sabotage*, *Men in Black II*, *The Adjustment Bureau*, and of course, *Ghostbusters II*.

10.

C. There are 20 answers on the Magic 8-Ball's icosahedron die (which has 20 sides), and only five of them are negative: "Don't count on it," "My reply is no," "My sources say no," "Outlook not so good," and "Very doubtful."

11. WHICH OF THE FOLLOWING IS NOT A REAL BEAUTY PAGEANT?

A. Miss Klingon Empire

B. Miss Artificial Beauty

C. The Armpit Queen

D. Miss Michael Jackson

12. HOW MANY BATHROOMS DOES THE WHITE HOUSE HAVE?

A. 22

B. 35

C. 50

D. 57

13. WHAT IS THE MOST COMMONLY REPORTED SUBJECT OF PEOPLE'S DREAMS?

A. Being chased

B. Falling/flying

C. Missing/failing an exam

D. Sex

11.

D. The Miss Klingon Empire beauty pageant is held every September at Dragon*Con in Atlanta. A Miss Artificial Beauty pageant was held in Beijing, China, in 2004; each contestant had to present doctor-certified proof of her surgical enhancements. Old Spice deodorant sponsors an annual pageant and festival in Battle Mountain, Nevada, which was once dubbed "the armpit of America" by humorist Gene Weingarten of the Washington Post. Sweaty T-shirt contests, deodorant throws, and a "quick-draw" antiperspirant contest lead up to the selection of the Armpit Queen.

12.

B. Encompassing approximately 55,000 square feet, the White House has 132 rooms, including 35 bathrooms and 16 family and guest rooms.

13.

A. It's often interpreted as symbolic of feeling as though you are being pursued by events or unpleasant emotions in your daily life.

14. JUPITER, MARS, MERCURY, NEPTUNE, PLUTO, AND VENUS ARE—OR WERE— PLANETS. (SORRY, PLUTO.) WHAT ELSE DO THESE NAMES HAVE IN COMMON?

15. WHICH IS NOT CONSIDERED ONE OF THE SEVEN HOLY VIRTUES?

A. Charity

B. Faith

C. Fortitude

D. Patience

16. WHAT IS DONALD DUCK'S MIDDLE NAME?

A. Buzz

B. Chesterfield

C. Fauntleroy

D. Fitzgerald

14.

Each is the name of a Roman god. Jupiter is the king of the gods; Mars is the god of war; Mercury is the messenger of the gods; Neptune is the god of the sea, earthquakes, and horses; Pluto is god of the dead and the Underworld; and Venus is the goddess of love and beauty.

15.

D. Whoever first uttered the adage "patience is a virtue" didn't know their holy virtues from a hole in the wall. The seven holy virtues are: faith, hope, charity, prudence, justice, temperance, and fortitude.

16.

C. "Fauntleroy" is a nice upper-class-sounding name, befitting a nephew of Scrooge McDuck, who has a fortune estimated at five billion impossibidillion fantasticatrillion dollars.

HISTORY

1. WHAT WAS THE END RESULT OF THE MANHATTAN PROJECT?

   A. An atomic bomb

   B. The Brooklyn Bridge

   C. A hovercraft

   D. The flux capacitor

2. THE WAR OF 1812 OCCURRED BETWEEN WHICH TWO NATIONS?

   A. France and Spain

   B. Russia and the British Empire

   C. The British Empire and the United States

   D. France and Russia

3. OF THE CELEBRATED GREEK PHILOSOPHERS —ARISTOTLE, PLATO, AND SOCRATES— WHO TAUGHT WHOM?

1.

A. The project lasted from 1942 to early 1947 and took place simultaneously in more than 30 cities in the United States, Canada, and the United Kingdom. Manhattan was the first headquarters of the top-secret project—right across from city hall.

2.

C. All the above pairings were at war with each other in 1812, due to a little emperor named Napoleon. Ultimately, the 32-month Revolutionary War rematch resolved the remaining concerns over the United States' declaration of independence, and the U.S. and the U.K. have been close allies ever since.

3.

Socrates taught Plato, and Plato taught Aristotle. You can remember the order by the acronym "SPA." Just don't confuse SPA with SAP or ASP.

4. **WHICH TOWN WAS THE SCENE OF THE GUNFIGHT AT THE O.K. CORRAL?**

A. Cimarron, New Mexico

B. Cripple Creek, Colorado

C. Dodge City, Kansas

D. Tombstone, Arizona

5. **WHAT AGE FOLLOWED THE BRONZE AGE?**

A. Ice Age

B. Iron Age

C. Stone Age

D. Age of Innocence

6. **DURING THEIR EXPEDITION ACROSS THE AMERICAN WEST FROM 1804 TO 1806, EXPLORERS MERIWETHER LEWIS AND WILLIAM CLARK TRAVELED WITH A FRENCH FUR TRADER AND HIS YOUNG SHOSHONE WIFE. WHAT WAS HER NAME?**

A. Kateri Tekakwitha

B. Pocahontas

C. Sacagawea

D. Weetamoo

4.

D. Actually, the famous gunfight between Wyatt Earp's crew and a group of outlaw brothers took place near the O.K. Corral, in an empty lot next to Camillus Fly's photography studio. Perhaps "Gunfight at the C.F. Studio" wasn't catchy enough.

5.

B. Characterized by the types of material being used to make tools at the time, the Stone Age is first in the Three-Age System of archaeology, followed by the Bronze Age and then the Iron Age. In Hollywood, though *Ice Age* was followed by *Ice Age: The Meltdown*, *Ice Age: Dawn of the Dinosaurs*, and *Ice Age: Continental Drift*.

6.

C. Although she did not serve as a guide for the expedition, as is often reported, Sacagawea helped foster diplomacy with Native Americans, provided input on the best routes to take, and served as an interpreter. She was the human version of a modern smart phone.

7. HOW MANY WIVES DID KING HENRY VIII HAVE?

A. 5

B. 6

C. 7

D. 8

8. HALLEY'S COMET LAST APPEARED IN 1986. WHEN IS IT SCHEDULED TO APPEAR NEXT?

A. 2041

B. 2048

C. 2061

D. 2087

9. ACCORDING TO THE SUPREME COURT DECISION IN THE CASE OF *BROWN V. BOARD OF EDUCATION*, THE *PLESSY V. FERGUSON* DECISION VIOLATED WHICH AMENDMENT BY UPHOLDING RACIAL SEGREGATION IN PUBLIC SCHOOLS?

A. First Amendment

B. Eleventh Amendment

C. Twelfth Amendment

D. Fourteenth Amendment

7.

B. Henry was married six times. Probably the most famous of his wives was the ill-fated Anne Boleyn, executed in 1536. If you have trouble keeping track of all of Henry's wives, try to remember this little mnemonic device: "Annulled, beheaded, died; annulled, beheaded, survived."

8.

C. The comet is visible from Earth every 75 to 76 years as it orbits the Sun. American author Mark Twain was born two weeks after the comet's perihelion (when it's closest to the sun) in 1835, and he predicted he would live until the comet's return. He died April 21, 1910—the day after the comet's next perihelion.

9.

D. The Equal Protection Clause of the Fourteenth Amendment states, "No state shall...deny to any person within its jurisdiction the equal protection of the laws." The Fifteenth Amendment ultimately allowed everyone to vote. (Except women—that happened 50 years later.)

10. WHAT WAS THE NAME OF THE THEATER WHERE PRESIDENT LINCOLN WAS ASSASSINATED?

A. Booth Theater

B. Ford's Theater

C. Lions Theater

D. Marquee Theater

11. INVESTMENT MANAGER BERNIE MADOFF SHOCKED WALL STREET AND THE WORLD WHEN HE WAS ARRESTED FOR STEALING BILLIONS OF DOLLARS FROM INVESTORS IN A MASSIVE FINANCIAL FRAUD. WHAT KIND OF SCAM WAS THIS?

12. WHICH WAR DO THE MOVIES *APOCALYPSE NOW*, *FULL METAL JACKET*, *HAMBURGER HILL*, AND *PLATOON* DEPICT?

A. Vietnam War

B. Korean War

C. Peloponnesian War

D. Crimean War

10.

B. On the night of April 14, 1865, John Wilkes Booth waited for the main character's big laugh line in Tom Taylor's play *Our American Cousin*: "Don't know the manners of good society, eh? Well, I guess I know enough to turn you inside out, old gal—you sockdologizing old man-trap." The audience's laughter concealed the gunshot. It's probably inappropriate to say you had to be there.

11.

A Ponzi scheme. U.S. prosecutors estimated that the worldwide scheme eventually totaled $64.8 billion. Madoff pled guilty to 11 criminal charges, including wire fraud, mail fraud, and money laundering. In 2009, he was sentenced to 150 years in prison. Using that length of sentence, he'll repay his duped investors at a rate of $14 per second...if he somehow manages to live until 2159.

12.

A. Including *Good Morning, Vietnam* would have made it too easy.

13. ALCATRAZ ISLAND HAS A RICH HISTORY, BEGINNING WITH ITS NAME. ALCATRAZ IS A SPANISH WORD THAT TRANSLATES INTO WHAT?

A. Prison

B. Pelican

C. Paradise

D. Poet

14. WHEN ALLIED TROOPS INVADED THE BEACHES OF NORMANDY, FRANCE, ON JUNE 6, 1944, IT WENT BY WHAT CODENAME?

A. Operation Neptune

B. Operation Luna

C. Operation Phalanx

D. Operation Eclipse

15. WHAT DID AL CAPONE GO TO JAIL FOR?

A. Extortion

B. Mail fraud

C. Tax evasion

D. Murder

13.

B. Originally considered the "Evil Island" by Native Americans, the "Island of the Pelicans" has been a military garrison, a military prison, the site of a Native American civil rights occupation, and a tourist trap. Operating as a federal prison from 1934 to 1963, Alcatraz housed such notorious figures as Al Capone, Mickey Cohen, and George "Machine Gun" Kelly. Now it's home to the California slender salamander. At least those don't try to escape.

14.

A. Likely named for the Roman god of the sea, Operation Neptune succeeded after elaborate deceptions led Adolf Hitler to believe that Allied forces planned to attack from the Straits of Dover. That operation was called Operation Bodyguard. No guessing where that name came from!

15.

C. Despite all his alleged wrongdoings, he was only ever convicted of income tax evasion in 1931 and sentenced to 11 years in prison. Capone was paroled in 1939 and succumbed to a heart attack in 1947.

16. WHO FAMOUSLY SAID, "THAT'S ONE SMALL STEP FOR [A] MAN, ONE GIANT LEAP FOR MANKIND"?

A. Buzz Aldrin

B. Neil Armstrong

C. John Glenn

D. Buzz Lightyear

17. HOW LONG WAS THE SHORTEST WAR IN HISTORY?

A. 16 months

B. 24 weeks

C. 32 days

D. 40 minutes

18. WHO WAS THE ONLY PRESIDENT TO GET MARRIED IN THE WHITE HOUSE?

A. Martin Van Buren

B. Grover Cleveland

C. James A. Garfield

D. Warren G. Harding

16.

B. Armstrong was the first man to walk on the moon. Later that year, Apollo 12 astronaut Pete Conrad, shortest member of his astronaut corps, landed on the Moon, jumped down from his lunar module, and said, "Whoopie! That may have been a small one for Neil, but it's a long one for me."

17.

D. After the pro-British sultan of Zanzibar died in 1896, a not-so-pro-British sultan took his place. The United Kingdom issued an ultimatum that resulted in a 40-minute war. Zanzibar took 500 casualties while Britain took just one. Another pro-British sultan assumed leadership of the puppet government, and Britain controlled Zanzibar for the next 67 years.

18.

B. Another noteworthy "one and only" fact about the man on the $1,000 bill: He's the only president to serve two non-consecutive terms. Cleveland was the 22nd and 24th president of the United States of America.

HUMAN BODY

1. EVERYONE KNOWS NOT TO LEAVE FINGERPRINTS BEHIND IF THEY WANT TO KEEP THEIR IDENTITY UNREVEALED. WHAT OTHER BODY PART HAS A UNIQUE PRINT?

A. Nose

B. Tongue

C. Ear

D. Elbow

2. WHAT IS THE COLORED PART OF THE EYE CALLED?

A. Cornea

B. Iris

C. Pupil

D. Retina

1.

B. Yet another reason not to lick doorknobs.

2.

B. The most common eye color in the world is brown. The least common is green. So what's the bestselling colored contact lens, you wonder? There's no record of that, but it's probably not cat's eyes.

3. **WHAT IS THE MOST COMMON BLOOD TYPE?**

A. B+

B. O-

C. AB

D. O+

4. **WHICH OF THESE IS A PIGMENT FOUND IN HUMAN SKIN THAT HELPS DEFEND AGAINST SUNBURN?**

A. Mitochondria

B. Miasma

C. Methylene

D. Melanin

5. **WHICH OF THE FOLLOWING BODY PARTS IS NO LONGER REQUIRED BY HUMANS?**

A. Vermiform appendix

B. Wisdom teeth

C. Auriclares muscles

D. Semilunar folds

79

3.

D. However, the O- blood type is the universal donor, meaning all other blood types can mix with it. That's why TV and movie doctors so often call for "O Neg." But people who have O- blood can only receive O- blood, and they make up less than 8% of the total U.S. population. To get an A+ on this blood test, you should also know that AB- is the rarest blood type—less than 1% of the total U.S. population has it.

4.

D. Melanin is found in most living organisms, but one major exception is spiders. With or without melanin, spiders make some people's skin crawl!

5.

All of the above. The vermiform appendix was probably your first guess, but wisdom teeth (leftovers from the era in which people chewed more foliage), auriclares muscles (those that redirect your ears), and semilunar folds (the fold in the corner of the eye, a vestigial remnant of another eyelid) are all nonessential in modern humans.

6. HAIR COLOR DETERMINES HOW MUCH ACTUAL HAIR IS ON YOUR HEAD. PUT THESE NATURAL HAIR COLORS IN ORDER, FROM THE COLOR THAT MEANS THE LEAST HAIR TO THE COLOR THAT MEANS THE MOST: BLONDE, RED, BLACK, AND BROWN.

7. WHAT IS THE NAME OF THE BONE THAT EXTENDS FROM THE SHOULDER TO THE ELBOW?

A. Humerus

B. Lunate

C. Radius

D. Ulna

8. WHAT NUTRIENT DO WE ABSORB FROM EXPOSURE TO SUNLIGHT?

A. Calcium

B. Magnesium

C. Vitamin A

D. Vitamin D

6.

Red (around 90,000), brown (around 100,000), black (around 110,000), and finally blonde (around 140,000). The average amount of hair follicles on the human head is 100,000, and each follicle produces about 20 new strands over time, so if you're already bald, scold your follicles for spending those strands so carelessly.

7.

A. The humerus is also known as the funny bone, and that's no joke. That last sentence was a joke, though. Did it tickle your humerus? (Not to be confused with humor, which is the fluid that fills your eyeballs.)

8.

D. Hence vitamin D's nickname: the sunshine vitamin. If you're looking to amp up your vitamin D intake, turn to mushrooms, fatty fish, beef liver, or eggs. Intake means you're supposed to eat them—not bask in their glow.

9. TRUE OR FALSE?

Humans have only five senses.

10. WE BEGIN OUR LIVES WITH MORE THAN 300 BONES, BUT SOME OF THOSE 300 FUSE TOGETHER DURING GROWTH. HOW MANY BONES DO ADULTS HAVE?

A. 182

B. 206

C. 274

D. 302

11. IF YOU HAVE *MAL DE MER*, WHAT ARE YOU SUFFERING FROM?

A. The flu

B. Food poisoning

C. Seasickness

D. Vertigo

9.

False. And there isn't an agreed-upon number of them, either. Aside from the main five (sight, sound, touch, taste, and smell), some of the others include: proprioception (knowing where your body parts are in relation to other parts), equilibrioception (balance), nociception (pain), thermoception (temperature), and, of course, hunger and thirst.

10.

C. Good thing bones don't continue to fuse—we wouldn't be much more flexible than Barbie and Ken dolls.

11.

C. It's French for seasickness. *Mal* means "bad" or "ill"; *de mer* means "of the sea." Now hand me a bucket, *s'il vous plait.*

12. TRUE OR FALSE?

To cure severe diarrhea in some patients, doctors have resorted to transplanting donor fecal matter.

13. IN 1955, JONAS SALK DISCOVERED A VACCINE FOR WHAT DISEASE?

A. Polio

B. Measles

C. Mumps

D. Rubella

14. WHICH ORGAN PRODUCES INSULIN?

A. Kidney

B. Liver

C. Pancreas

D. Small intestine

15. WHAT SYMPTOM DOES *PILOERECTION* CAUSE?

A. Excessive blinking

B. Goosebumps

C. Impotence

D. Vomiting

12.

True. There's a bacterium called *Clostridium difficile* ("C. diff") that can overtake the intestines. The only way to restore the good bacteria required to defeat the bad is to use a healthy person's bacteria.

13.

A. Incredibly, Salk chose not to patent the vaccine. On his decision, Salk said: "There is no patent. Could you patent the sun?"

14.

C. Insulin is a hormone that moves sugar out of the blood and into the body's cells. You can think of it as a key that unlocks the door to the cell so that food (sugar/glucose) can get inside and feed it. A deficiency of insulin can lead to diabetes.

15.

B. *Piloerection* is an involuntary reflex that causes the muscles around the base of each hair follicle to contract, making the hairs stand up and causing small bumps to appear.

16. **WHAT IS THE LARGEST ORGAN IN THE HUMAN BODY?**

A. Brain

B. Lower intestine

C. Lungs

D. Skin

17. **HOW MANY CHROMOSOME PAIRS CAN BE FOUND IN A HUMAN CELL?**

A. 11

B. 16

C. 20

D. 23

18. **WHERE IN OR ON YOUR BODY IS THE HALLUX FOUND?**

A. Ear

B. Face

C. Foot

D. Reproductive organs

16.

D. The average person sheds nearly 1.5 pounds of skin per year. After 50 years, you'll have left 75 pounds of old skin lying around! Try and shed that image.

17.

D. Chromosomes are made of DNA. Half of your chromosomes come from your mother, the other half from your father. And it's the 23rd chromosome that determines your sex. One X always comes from Mom; X or Y comes from Dad. XX: it's a girl! XY: it's a boy! And the double helix of life rolls on and on.

18.

C. *Hallux* means big toe; *pollex* means thumb; *Horcrux* means you think too much about the Harry Potter books and films.

1. WHO IS ANGELINA JOLIE'S FAMOUS DAD?

A. James Caan

B. George Hamilton

C. Harvey Keitel

D. Jon Voight

2. WHO IS THE OLDEST ACTOR EVER TO WIN AN OSCAR?

A. George Burns

B. Kirk Douglas

C. Paul Newman

D. Christopher Plummer

1.

D. The two haven't always been on the best of terms, but they allegedly reconciled in 2010. Mom was actress Marcheline Bertrand.

2.

D. Plummer was 82 years old when he scored the Best Supporting Actor statuette for his role in the 2011 film *Beginners*.

3. CAN YOU TELL WHICH OF THESE IS NOT THE TITLE OF A REAL MOVIE?

A. *Cannibal Cousin and the Knife of Destiny*

B. *Sorority Babes in the Slimeball Bowl-O-Rama*

C. *Pumpkinhead II: Blood Wings*

D. *Mari-Cookie and the Killer Tarantula in 8 Legs to Love You*

4. THE JAMES BOND SERIES IS FAMOUS FOR ITS GORGEOUS LEADING LADIES. CAN YOU MATCH THE BOND GIRL WITH THE MOVIE IN WHICH SHE APPEARED?

1. *Goldfinger*   **A.** Jinx Johnson

2. *You Only Live Twice*   **B.** Kissy Suzuki

3. *Quantum of Solace*   **C.** Pussy Galore

4. *Casino Royale*   **D.** Strawberry Fields

5. *Die Another Day*   **E.** Vesper Lynd

5. WHAT IS THE ONLY X-RATED MOVIE EVER TO WIN AN ACADEMY AWARD FOR BEST PICTURE?

3.

A. Actress Linnea Quigley, known as the "Queen of Scream," starred in the other three (1988, 1994, and 1998, respectively), among other piquantly titled horror thrillers. The titles may be more screamworthy than the movies!

4.

1. C; 2. B; 3. D; 4. E; 5. A.

5.

Midnight Cowboy. The movie, starring Dustin Hoffman and Jon Voight, took home the prize in 1969. Because of the growing stigma associated with X ratings, the film's rating was changed to R in 1971 without anything being changed or removed.

6. THERE ARE MORE THAN 2,400 STARS ON THE HOLLYWOOD WALK OF FAME. WHICH OF THESE MAJOR HOLLYWOOD SUPERSTARS DOES NOT HAVE ONE?

A. Clint Eastwood

B. Harrison Ford

C. Arnold Schwarzenegger

D. John Travolta

7. IN *STAR WARS*, WHAT IS THE NAME OF HAN SOLO'S SPACECRAFT?

A. *Apollo*

B. *Enterprise*

C. *Millennium Falcon*

D. *Voyager*

8. IN THE *BACK TO THE FUTURE* FRANCHISE, AT WHAT SPEED IS THE DELOREAN TIME MACHINE ACTIVATED?

A. 78 mph

B. 88 mph

C. 98 mph

D. 108 mph

6.

A. Go ahead—give Eastwood a star. It would probably make his day.

7.

C. The Falcon's design was allegedly inspired by a hamburger, with the cockpit being an olive on the side. Mmmm-mm. Hungry?

8.

B. Hello? McFly? Is anybody home? Of course you knew that the flux capacitor kicks into gear at 88 miles per hour.

9. WHO PLAYED INDIANA JONES'S FATHER IN *INDIANA JONES AND THE TEMPLE OF DOOM*?

A. Sean Connery

B. James Garner

C. Gene Hackman

D. Peter O'Toole

10. WHICH OF THE FOLLOWING JULIA ROBERTS MOVIES WAS NOT BASED ON A TRUE STORY?

A. *Charlie Wilson's War* (2007)

B. *Eat Pray Love* (2010)

C. *Erin Brockovich* (2000)

D. *Larry Crowne* (2011)

11. WHICH FAMOUS *SATURDAY NIGHT LIVE* ALUM WROTE 2004'S HIT FILM *MEAN GIRLS*?

A. Tina Fey

B. Ana Gasteyer

C. Amy Poehler

D. Maya Rudolph

9.

A. Yep, James Bond himself was also Indy's dad. Director Steven Spielberg thought Connery was an obvious choice for the role, as Bond was an inspiration for Indiana's character.

10.

D. Don't get Charlie Wilson confused with Larry Crowne. Both movies costarred Tom Hanks; only one of them was the story of a real person (Wilson).

11.

A. Gasteyer and Poehler each had a role in the film, but Fey wrote the script. Poehler played the mom of Rachel McAdams's mean-girl character, which was odd because in real life she's just seven years older than McAdams.

12. MARILYN MONROE IN A BILLOWING WHITE DRESS OVER A SUBWAY GRATE—WHO DOESN'T KNOW THAT SCENE? BUT DO YOU KNOW WHAT MOVIE IT'S FROM?

A. *Gentlemen Prefer Blondes*

B. *How to Marry a Millionaire*

C. *The Seven Year Itch*

D. *Some Like It Hot*

13. WHICH OSCAR-NOMINATED ACTION STAR IS ALSO A SEASONED HELICOPTER PILOT AND REAL-LIFE HERO?

A. Tom Cruise

B. Harrison Ford

C. John Travolta

D. Denzel Washington

14. WHICH TWO ACTORS STARRED IN 2005'S *BROKEBACK MOUNTAIN*?

97

12.

C. The pose is so famous, in fact, that it was commemorated with a 26-foot-tall statue on Chicago's Magnificent Mile. Sadly, the statue was only a temporary display.

13.

B. Ford has twice rescued stranded hikers in his Bell 407 helicopter. In July 2000 he airlifted a hiker off Table Mountain in Idaho, and a year later he rescued a 13-year-old Boy Scout who had gotten lost in Yellowstone Park.

14.

Jake Gyllenhaal and Heath Ledger. Both were nominated for Academy Awards.

15. BRAT PACK MOVIES *THE BREAKFAST CLUB, FERRIS BUELLER'S DAY OFF*, AND *SIXTEEN CANDLES* (ALL DIRECTED BY JOHN HUGHES) WERE SET IN THE SUBURBS OF WHICH METROPOLIS?

A. Boston

B. Chicago

C. Los Angeles

D. Philadelphia

16. WHICH ACTOR PROVIDES THE VOICE OF *TOY STORY*'S BUZZ LIGHTYEAR?

A. Tim Allen

B. Will Ferrell

C. Tom Hanks

D. Mike Myers

17. WHICH ACTRESS PLAYED GERTIE IN THE MOVIE *E.T. THE EXTRA-TERRESTRIAL*?

A. Drew Barrymore

B. Cameron Diaz

C. Gwyneth Paltrow

D. Reese Witherspoon

15.

B. It seems there was no place like home for Hughes, who grew up in Northbrook, Illinois, a suburb of Chicago.

16.

A. You're sure to recognize the other actors' voices from animated films as well: Will Ferrell plays Megamind, Tom Hanks is the voice of Buzz's pal Woody, and Mike Myers is Shrek.

17.

A. Barrymore was just seven years old when she starred in the blockbuster movie.

100

18. **IN 1999'S** *OFFICE SPACE,* **THE MEEK AND MUMBLY MILTON IS OBSESSED WITH WHICH OFFICE SUPPLY?**

A. Calculator

B. Scissors

C. Stapler

D. Wite-Out

19. **WHICH OF THE FOLLOWING ACTORS FROM THE** *STAR WARS* **FILM SERIES WAS A STEP-COUSIN TO IAN FLEMING, AUTHOR OF THE JAMES BOND NOVELS?**

A. Alec Guinness (Obi-Wan Kenobi)

B. Anthony Daniels (C-3PO)

C. Liam Neeson (Qui-Gon Jinn)

D. Christopher Lee (Count Dooku)

20. **TRUE OR FALSE?**

In *Friday the 13th Part II*, Jason Voorhees' mask was based on a 1950s Detroit Red Wings goalie mask.

18.

C. Milton's all about his Swingline stapler. Well, that and burning down the building.

19.

D. Lee's mother married into Fleming's family, but it was his acting that got him a part as the James Bond villain Scaramanga in *The Man with the Golden Gun*, right? Maybe. Lee was Fleming's regular golf partner after all. Do you think he ever golfed with George Lucas?

20.

False, but not for the reason you think. It *was* based on goaltender Terry Sawchuk's mask from the Red Wings—but Jason didn't wear it until *Friday the 13th Part III*.

MUSIC

1. BY WHICH NAME WAS WILL SMITH KNOWN DURING HIS EARLY RAP CAREER?

2. WHO WAS SMITH'S HIP-HOP COLLABORATOR (AND OCCASIONAL TV FRIEND)?

3. WHICH OF THE FOLLOWING SINGERS GOT HIS STAGE NAME FROM A BILLBOARD ADVERTISING A HEARING-AID RETAILER?

A. Sting

B. Prince

C. Bono

D. Moby

4. HOW MANY KEYS ARE ON A STANDARD PIANO KEYBOARD?

1.

The Fresh Prince. He later starred on the TV show *The Fresh Prince of Bel-Air* (1990–96). At the time, few people would have predicted that the rapper would eventually be Oscar-nominated (*Ali*, 2001, and *The Pursuit of Happyness*, 2006).

2.

DJ Jazzy Jeff

3.

C. As the story goes, Bono (Paul David Hewson) was inspired by a Dublin hearing-aid shop called Bono Vox—Latin for "good voice."

4.

88 (52 white, 36 black)

5. GERMAN COMPOSER LUDWIG VAN BEETHOVEN BEGAN TO LOSE HIS SENSE OF WHAT WHEN HE WAS **28** YEARS OLD?

A. Hearing

B. Humor

C. Sight

D. Style

6. A HOST OF MUSICAL GENIUSES HAVE GONE TO AN EARLY GRAVE. BRIAN JONES (A FOUNDING MEMBER OF THE ROLLING STONES), JIMI HENDRIX, JANIS JOPLIN, JIM MORRISON, KURT COBAIN, AND AMY WINEHOUSE ALL PASSED AWAY AT THE SAME YOUNG AGE. HOW OLD WERE THEY?

7. OZZY OSBOURNE BECAME FAMOUS WITH WHICH HEAVY METAL BAND?

A. AC/DC

B. Black Sabbath

C. Iron Maiden

D. Judas Priest

5.

A. At around age 28, Beethoven developed a severe case of tinnitus and began to lose his hearing. This did not affect his ability to compose music, but it made conducting concerts increasingly difficult. According to one story, at the premiere of his Ninth Symphony when he was 54 years old, he had to be turned around to see the applause of the audience because he couldn't hear it.

6.

They were 27. If you're a rock star and you're about to turn 27, you might want to consider taking a year off.

7.

B. B is for Black Sabbath, but it's also for bat—as in the bat whose head Ozzy legendarily bit off when a fan tossed it onto the stage at a 1982 concert.

8. PUT THESE *AMERICAN IDOL* WINNERS IN ORDER FROM EARLIEST TO MOST RECENT.

A. Phillip Phillips

B. Fantasia Barrino

C. David Cook

D. Jordin Sparks

E. Carrie Underwood

9. WHICH *AMERICAN IDOL* CONTESTANT HAS WON AN ACADEMY AWARD?

10. WHAT EVENTUALLY KILLED THE OLD LADY WHO SWALLOWED THE FLY?

A. A cow

B. A fly

C. A horse

D. A moose

11. TRUE OR FALSE?

Michael Jackson's "Thriller" video was nominated for an Academy Award.

8.

B. (Season 3), E. (Season 4), D. (Season 6), C. (Season 7), A. (Season 11)

9.

Jennifer Hudson (Best Supporting Actress 2006, *Dreamgirls*)

10.

C. A horse, of course!

11.

False. It wasn't nominated, but producers made sure it was eligible by giving it a one-week theatrical release in 1983, opening for the Disney movie *Fantasia*. Parents weren't too thrilled about their toddlers getting an eyeful of zombie action.

12. WHICH COUNTRY SINGER IS KNOWN AS THE MAN IN BLACK?

A. Clint Black

B. Garth Brooks

C. Johnny Cash

D. Hank Williams

13. CAN YOU NAME THE SONG EACH OF THESE LYRICS COMES FROM?

A. "Thunderbolt and lightning, very, very frightening."

B. "A singer in a smoky room, a smell of wine and cheap perfume."

C. "Hands, touching hands, reaching out, touching me, touching you."

D. "Well, I know that you're in love with him, 'cause I saw you dancin' in the gym."

E. "You start to scream, but terror takes the sound before you make it."

14. CAN YOU NAME THE FIVE ORIGINAL MTV VJS?

12.

C. Cash has been inducted into the Country Music Hall of Fame, the Rock and Roll Hall of Fame, the Gospel Music Hall of Fame, and the Rockabilly Hall of Fame.

13.

A. "Bohemian Rhapsody" (Queen)

B. "Don't Stop Believin'" (Journey)

C. "Sweet Caroline" (Neil Diamond)

D. "American Pie" (Don McLean)

E. "Thriller" (Michael Jackson)

14.

Alan Hunter, Mark Goodman, Nina Blackwood, Martha Quinn, and J. J. Jackson (who passed away in 2004). Nowadays, you can find the remaining VJs introducing 1980s hits 24 hours a day, 7 days a week on satellite radio...just like how they did it on MTV, when it still stood for Music Television.

15. **WHO IS THE GREEK GOD OF MUSIC?**

A. Apollo

B. Dionysus

C. Hermes

D. Zeus

16. **WHICH LEGENDARY JAZZ MUSICIAN WAS KNOWN AS "SATCHMO"?**

A. Duke Ellington

B. Charlie Parker

C. Glenn Miller

D. Louis Armstrong

17. **LIONEL RICHIE ORIGINALLY RECORDED "ENDLESS LOVE" AS A DUET WITH DIANA ROSS. ON HIS 2012 ALBUM *TUSKEGEE*, HE RECORDED A NEW VERSION WITH WHICH COUNTRY SINGER?**

A. Faith Hill

B. Taylor Swift

C. Natalie Maines

D. Shania Twain

15.

A. Apollo was not only the god of music—he was also the god of healing, the sun, and poetry, to name a few. If you got this question right, lift your glass to Dionysus, god of wine, parties, and festivals.

16.

D. When Armstrong was a child, his friends called him Satchelmouth because they thought his mouth was as large as a satchel. (He was also sometimes called Gatemouth. With friends like that, who needs enemies?) A music journalist mispronounced the moniker, shortening it to "Satchmo." Armstrong loved the name and quickly adopted it.

17.

D. Richie's tenth studio album is comprised of his old hit songs reinterpreted as duets. Some guests include Willie Nelson, Darius Rucker of Hootie and the Blowfish, and Jimmy Buffett. Wisely, he chose not to include his daughter Nicole's friend Paris Hilton.

18. MANY FAMOUS ROCK 'N' ROLL BANDS WENT BY DIFFERENT NAMES BEFORE THEY MADE IT BIG. CAN YOU IDENTIFY THE FORMER NAMES OF THESE BANDS?

1. The Beatles **A.** Feedback; The Hype

2. Journey **B.** Golden Gate Rhythm Section

3. KISS **C.** The Pendletones

4. The Rolling Stones **D.** Satan's Jesters

5. U2 **E.** Wicked Lester

19. WHICH CD WAS THE FIRST ONE MANUFACTURED IN THE U.S.?

A. Billy Joel's *52nd Street*

B. Bruce Springsteen's *Born in the U.S.A.*

C. Cyndi Lauper's *She's So Unusual*

D. Blondie's *The Hunter*

18.

1. C; 2. B; 3. E; 4. D; 5. A.

19.

B. Joel's 1978 album was the first to be available for sale on CD in Japan in 1982, but Springsteen's most iconic album was aptly named—it was the first made in the U.S.A. starting in September 1984.

TELEVISION

1. **WHICH COMEDIAN FAMOUSLY RIFFED ABOUT THE "SEVEN WORDS YOU CAN NEVER SAY ON TELEVISION" WAY BACK IN 1972?**

A. Bill Cosby

B. Sam Kinison

C. Richard Pryor

D. George Carlin

2. **WHICH FORMER PRESIDENT WAS INVITED TO MAKE A GUEST APPEARANCE ON THE SERIES FINALE OF *CHEERS*?**

A. Bill Clinton

B. George H. W. Bush

C. Ronald Reagan

D. Jimmy Carter

1.

D. These days, you can actually say one of the dirty words on network television and three of them on basic cable. But of course, all of them regularly appear on premium cable, and none of them will appear here.

2.

A. President Clinton passed on the offer, so a different type of president took his place—Brandon Tartikoff (then head of NBC programming). He was joined by cartoonist Garry Trudeau in cameos for the final episode, which aired May 20, 1993.

3. WHICH FAMOUS *SATURDAY NIGHT LIVE* ALUM GOT HER START ON THE REALITY SHOW *THE JOE SCHMO SHOW*?

A. Amy Poehler

B. Kristen Wiig

C. Tina Fey

D. Maya Rudolph

4. WHICH OF THE FOLLOWING SUPERSTARS GOT HIS START ON TV, MAKING GUEST APPEARANCES IN *ANOTHER WORLD*, *GROWING PAINS*, *DALLAS*, AND *21 JUMP STREET*?

A. Leonardo DiCaprio

B. Johnny Depp

C. Brad Pitt

D. George Clooney

5. WHAT IS THE NAME OF THE HOLIDAY CELEBRATION COINED ON THE TV SHOW *SEINFELD*?

3.

B. Spike TV's reality show was about one guy that didn't realize he was on a fake reality show. Wiig was one of the actors in on the scam, as was David Hornsby. You might know him better as Rickety Cricket on *It's Always Sunny in Philadelphia*. Not too shabby for two former Joe Schmos.

4.

C. DiCaprio had a major role near the end of *Growing Pains'* run, and Depp was the main attraction on *21 Jump Street*, but Pitt was a guest star on all those shows. He also appeared on *Friends* as a former classmate of Jennifer Aniston's Rachel. Were you aware that they used to be married in real life?

5.

Festivus. Those looking to celebrate the "Festivus for the Rest of Us" should plan on the traditional "Airing of Grievances" and "Feats of Strength," in which the head of household must be pinned in a wrestling match. An unadorned aluminum pole is put up instead of a Christmas tree.

6. IN THE TELEVISION SHOW *PARKS AND RECREATION*, THE FICTIONAL CITY OF PAWNEE IS LOCATED IN WHAT STATE?

A. Ohio

B. Pennsylvania

C. Iowa

D. Indiana

7. MATCH THESE TV SERIES TO THE CITIES IN WHICH THEY ARE SET.

1. *CSI: Crime Scene Investigation*

2. *Grey's Anatomy*

3. *House*

4. *Law & Order (the original)*

5. *NCIS*

A. Las Vegas

B. New York City

C. Princeton, New Jersey

D. Seattle

E. Washington, D.C.

6.

D. Councilwoman Leslie Knope, as portrayed by Amy Poehler, truly loves the city of Pawnee. Her husband is a close second...or maybe waffles are.

7.

1. A; 2. D; 3. C; 4. B; 5. E.

A trivia tidbit for you: There have been four American spin-offs of the original *Law and Order*: *Special Victims Unit*, *Criminal Intent*, *Trial by Jury*, and *L.A.* Versions of the show have also been produced in Russia, France, and the United Kingdom.

8. *STAR TREK* HAS HAD MANY INCARNATIONS ON TELEVISION. WHICH RUN HAD THE MOST EPISODES?

A. *The Original Series*

B. *The Next Generation*

C. *Deep Space Nine*

D. *Voyager*

E. *Enterprise*

9. WHEN WAS THE FIRST-EVER TELEVISED BASEBALL GAME?

A. 1939

B. 1951

C. 1948

D. 1942

10. WHICH OF THESE ACTORS WAS NEVER A PART OF THE *SATURDAY NIGHT LIVE* CAST?

A. Alec Baldwin

B. Robert Downey, Jr.

C. Will Ferrell

D. Adam Sandler

8.

B. It was close, but *The Next Generation* aired 178 episodes, plus four theatrical films. *Deep Space Nine* aired 176, *Voyager* aired 172, and *Enterprise* aired 98. *Star Trek: The Original Series* had only 79 episodes, but it did get four spin-off series, plus eight movies (and counting). Captain Kirk for the win!

9.

A. On May 17, 1939, the game between Princeton and Columbia was played at Baker Field and broadcast on W2XBS. Princeton won 2-1, but we all know TV really won.

10.

A. As of 2016, Baldwin has hosted *SNL* a record 16 times, but he was never a cast member.

11. JON STEWART MADE A GLOBAL IMPACT AS HOST OF *THE DAILY SHOW* ON COMEDY CENTRAL, AND THE SHOW HELPED LAUNCH THE CAREERS OF SEVERAL FORMER CAST MEMBERS AS WELL. WHICH OF THE FOLLOWING FUNNY FOLKS DID NOT GET HIS OR HER START ON *THE DAILY SHOW*?

A. Steve Carell

B. Stephen Colbert

C. Ed Helms

D. Amy Sedaris

12. ACTOR IWAN RHEON PLAYS THIS CHARACTER ON THE GAME OF THRONES, BUT HE ALMOST PLAYED THIS CHARACTER INSTEAD.

A. Ramsay Bolton; Jon Snow

B. Jaime Lannister; Tyrion Lannister

C. Ramsay Bolton; Tywin Lannister

D. Jon Snow; Ned Stark

11.

D. The actress, comedian, and author has appeared on Stewart's show as a guest, but she was never a regular contributor.

12.

A. Rheon plays hateful character Ramsay Bolton, but he auditioned for the part of Jon Snow. Kit Harrington won the part.

13. **WHO COHOSTED THE FIRST SEASON OF**
AMERICAN IDOL WITH RYAN SEACREST?

A. Brian Dunkleman

B. Jason Kennedy

C. Ben Lyons

D. Catt Sadler

14. **WHAT ARE THE NAMES OF THE TWO**
OLD MEN WHO SIT IN THE BALCONY
ON _THE MUPPET SHOW_?

A. Aspin and Ludsthorp

B. Chilton and Gerard

C. Hawkins and Nigel

D. Waldorf and Statler

15. **PUT THESE REALITY SHOWS IN THE ORDER**
IN WHICH THEY DEBUTED, FIRST TO LAST:

A. _American Idol_

B. _Dancing with the Stars_

C. _The Real World_

D. _Survivor_

E. _Top Chef_

13.

A. Dunkleman left the show after the first season with his career in ruins. Seacrest went on to become an entertainment mogul.

14.

D. The ornery octogenarians enjoy heckling the other Muppets from the best seats in the house. Their names are based on hotels in New York: the Waldorf–Astoria and the Statler Hilton.

15.

C. (1992); **D.** (2000); **A.** (2002); **B.** (2005); **E.** (2006)

16. WHAT NAME DID THE CORE GROUP OF FRIENDS USE TO REFER TO THEMSELVES ON THE SERIES *BUFFY THE VAMPIRE SLAYER* (1997–2003)?

A. The Badanovs

B. The Felix Faith

C. The Scooby Gang

D. The Underdog Squad

17. TGIF WAS ABC'S FRIDAY NIGHT BLOCK OF FAMILY-FRIENDLY SITCOMS. WHICH OF THESE SHOWS WAS NEVER UNDER THE "THANK GOODNESS IT'S FUNNY" BRAND?

A. *Perfect Strangers*

B. *Dinosaurs*

C. *Webster*

D. *Hangin' with Mr. Cooper*

16.

C. Buffy, Willow, Xander, and Giles formed the core of the Scooby Gang, or the Scoobies. The spooky goings-on in Sunnydale, California, influenced today's vampire, werewolf, and supernatural craze.

17.

C. TGIF started in 1989, and although *Webster* aired on Fridays in 1987, it moved elsewhere on the schedule to make room for *Full House* the next year. The first official set of shows included *Full House*, *Family Matters*, *Perfect Strangers*, and *Just the Ten of Us*. How many of their theme songs can you still sing?